D1517729

FITNESS MATH

KATIE MARSICO

Lerner Publications ◆ Minneapolis

To Nico Filice—one of the bravest boys I know

Lerner Publications Company
A division of Lerner Publishing Group, Inc.
241 First Avenue North
Minneapolis, MN 55401 USA

For reading levels and more information, look up this title at www.lernerbooks.com.

Photo Acknowledgments
The images in this book are used with the permission of: © iStockphoto.com/rusm, p. 1 (grid paper); © iStockphoto.com/chictype, p. 1 (shoes); © Svetlana Braun/Getty Images, p. 4; © Donald Pye/Alamy, p. 5; © iStockphoto.com/spxChrome, pp. 6, 7, 9, 10, 12, 13, 17, 19, 21, 27 (notebook); © iStockphoto.com/tarasov_vl, p. 6 (bike); © iStockphoto.com/snappy_girl, p. 7 (jump rope); © Tetra Images/Alamy, p. 8; © Laura Westlund/Independent Picture Service, p. 9 (map); © Stockbyte/Getty Images, p. 10 (candy); © Cultura Creative/Alamy, p. 11; © vstock24/Shutterstock.com, p. 12 (stopwatch); © iStockphoto.com/alubalish, pp. 13, 17, 19, 27 (torn paper); © iStockphoto.com/Rouzes, p. 13 (cake topper); © Bigshots/Getty Images, p. 14; © iStockphoto.com/SashaFoxWalters, p. 15; © Ariel Skelley/Blend Images/Getty Images, p. 16; © iStockphoto.com/GlobalIP, p. 17 (dog); © iStockphoto.com/gbh007, p. 18; © iStockphoto.com/Ziviani, p. 19 (stopwatch); © Lane Oatey/Blue Jean Images/Getty Images, p. 20; © iStockphoto.com/zimmytws, p. 21 (racket and ball); © Thomas Barwick/Getty Images, p. 22; © iStockphoto.com/Cybernesco, p. 23; © Rob Lewine/Getty Images, p. 24; © iStockphoto.com/larkyphoto, p. 25; © Gary S. Chapman/Getty Images, p. 26; © iStockphoto.com/kravcs, p. 27 (backpack); © Tetra Images/Alamy, p. 28.

Front Cover: © Jessie Jean/The Image Bank/Getty Images (girl), © iStockphoto.com/rusm (grid paper).
Back Cover: © iStockphoto/Nastco (ball), © iStockphoto.com/jocic.

Main body text set in Conduit ITC Std Medium 14/18. Typeface provided by International Typeface Corp.

Library of Congress Cataloging-in-Publication Data

Marsico, Katie, 1980- author.
     Fitness math / by Katie Marsico.
       pages   cm. — (Math everywhere!)
     Includes bibliographical references and index.
     ISBN 978-1-4677-8578-5 (lb : alk. paper) — ISBN 978-1-4677-8628-7 (pb : alk. paper) — ISBN 978-1-4677-8629-4 (eb pdf)
     1. Mathematics—Juvenile literature. 2. Physical fitness—Mathematics—Juvenile literature. 3. Word problems (Mathematics)—Juvenile literature. I. Title.
     QA40.5.M3772 2016
     513—dc23   2014041406

Manufactured in the United States of America
1 – CG – 7/15/15

TABLE OF CONTENTS

ALREADY ACTIVE

It's time to break a sweat! Gym shoes? Check! Water bottle? Check! Calculator? Wait, what does math have to do with physical fitness? A lot! Math makes it easier to exercise; eat well; and be an active, healthy person. Want proof? Well, then, let's get moving!

That's what Claire is hoping to do. Last week, she signed up for a fitness class with her friends. It sounded like fun, but she's having second thoughts. She doesn't play sports, and she's never worked out in a gym. Claire worries she's not physically active enough to take the class.

Not so fast! Ms. Vargas, the instructor, reminds Claire that people take classes to learn new things. In this class, Claire will learn to become more fit. Plus, Ms. Vargas guesses that Claire may be more physically active than she realizes.

Fitness experts recommend that most kids participate in *at least* 60 minutes of physical activity each day. Ms. Vargas points out there are many different ways to do this. Not all of them happen in a gym, on a field, or even in a fitness class! A walk around the block, a game of tag, and climbing a tree all get a person's heart going.

Today is Wednesday. Ms. Vargas tells Claire to think back to Sunday. She asks Claire to record her physical activity for the past three days in the table below:

Claire's Daily Physical Activity		
Sunday	**Monday**	**Tuesday**
Walked the dog/10 mins.	Walked to school/5 mins.	Walked to school/5 mins.
Played tug-of-war at a family picnic/15 mins.	Jumped rope with friends/15 mins.	Played volleyball during gym/20 mins.
Rode my bike with a friend/25 mins.	Walked home from school/5 mins.	Swung on the monkey bars at recess/15 mins.
	Chased my little brother around the house before bed/10 mins.	Walked to a friend's house after school/10 mins.

Ms. Vargas and Claire review the table together. Ms. Vargas explains that Claire's average amount of daily physical activity = the total number of minutes she's physically active ÷ the number of days that include physical activity. **What's Claire's average amount of daily physical activity for this time span? Based on this average, what percentage of her *recommended* daily physical activity is Claire getting?** (Hint: percentage = actual amount ÷ recommended amount.)

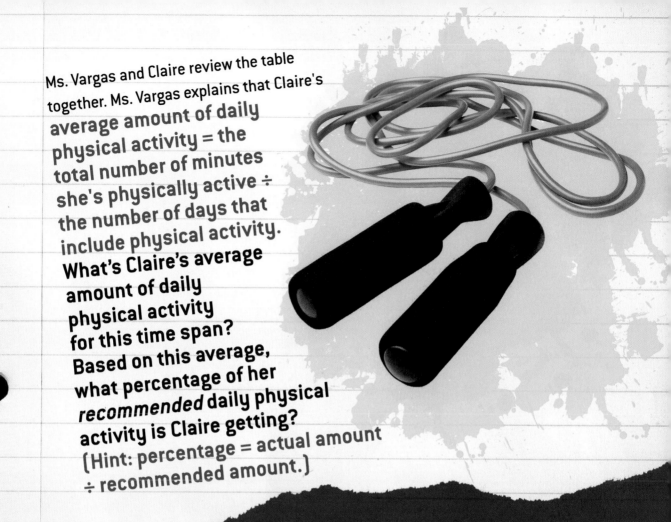

DO THE MATH!

Is the elevator out of order? Even if it's working, think about taking the stairs! Walking up and down stairs is an easy way to fit in daily physical activity. Let's say you live on the fourth floor of an apartment building. There's an elevator, but you'd rather use the stairs. There are 12 steps between each floor, including between the ground level and the first floor. At about 7:30 a.m., you leave for school. On the way home, you decide to do homework with your friend. She lives on the sixth floor of your building. Later, you head downstairs to grab your violin from your bedroom. Then you race to your violin teacher's studio on the seventh floor. Finally, you head back to your place for dinner. How many stair steps have you walked up or down in your apartment building today?

Check your answers to all questions on pages 30–31.

FITNESS OR HALLOWEEN FUN?

Trick-or-treat! For most kids, Halloween is about costumes and candy. Yet it's also an excellent opportunity to get moving. Walking from house to house on October 31 is a form of physical activity. And the more ground trick-or-treaters cover, the more candy they're likely to collect!

Marc and Nina have this in mind as they leave their house at the northwest corner of Elm and Acorn Streets. (Check out a map of their neighborhood below.) Their dad walks with them as they ring all the doorbells on both sides of Elm.

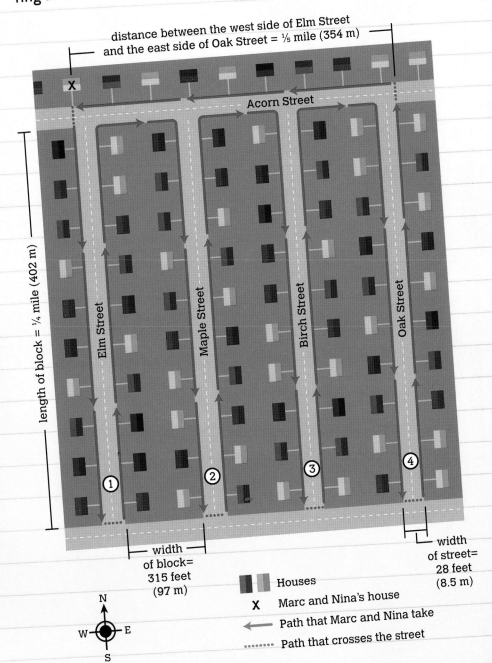

distance between the west side of Elm Street and the east side of Oak Street = ⅛ mile (354 m)

Acorn Street

Elm Street

Maple Street

Birch Street

Oak Street

length of block = ¼ mile (402 m)

width of block = 315 feet (97 m)

width of street = 28 feet (8.5 m)

Houses

X   Marc and Nina's house

←   Path that Marc and Nina take

......   Path that crosses the street

N
W · E
S

Marc and Nina do the same thing on three other blocks—Maple, Birch, and Oak. Each block is ¼ miles (402 meters) long. As they wind their way east, they cross a total of four streets. The width of a street in Marc's and Nina's neighborhood is about 28 feet (8.5 m). The width of each block, or the space between streets, is 315 feet (97 m).

Marc and Nina finally head home after walking up the east side of Oak Street. They cross a fifth street—Acorn Street—and travel west. The distance between eastern Oak and western Elm is about 0.2 miles (354 m). **How many miles have Marc and Nina walked in their quest for candy?**
(Hint: 1 mile [1.6 kilometers] = 5,280 feet [1,600m])

MOVE TO THE MUSIC!

Thump, thump, thump. Is that the beat of the music or Gwen's heart pounding? She turns off her MP3 player and sips some water. Gwen adores dancing! Is it helping her stay fit, though? How can Gwen tell if she's doing an intense workout or simply moving to the music?

Mom says she can answer that question by taking Gwen's pulse. A pulse, or heart rate, shows how fast someone's heart is beating. The heart rate speeds up during physical activity. Intense exercise strengthens the heart by making it work harder.

Before taking Gwen's pulse, Mom grabs her stopwatch. Meanwhile, Gwen dances to a few more songs. When the last one ends, Mom gently presses her fingers along Gwen's inner wrist. She searches for a steady beat. Next, Mom sets the stopwatch for 10 seconds. During that time, she counts the number of beats she feels—25.

Gwen's mom says that **heart rate = pulse beats per minute (bpm)**. Gwen knows that **1 minute = 60 seconds**. So, **heart rate = pulse beats per 10-second period × 6**.

Mom also explains that maximum heart rate is the fastest someone's heart can safely beat while working its hardest. **Maximum heart rate = 220 bpm – a person's age.** Meanwhile, target heart rate is how fast someone's heart should beat during an effective workout. **Target heart rate = 50 to 85 percent of a person's maximum heart rate.**

Anything less than the target heart rate means exercise should be more intense. Anything more than the target heart rate means the heart is being overworked. Gwen is 10 years old. **Is moving to the music a safe, effective way for her to be physically active? In other words, is she within her target heart rate as she dances?** Round to the nearest whole bpm.

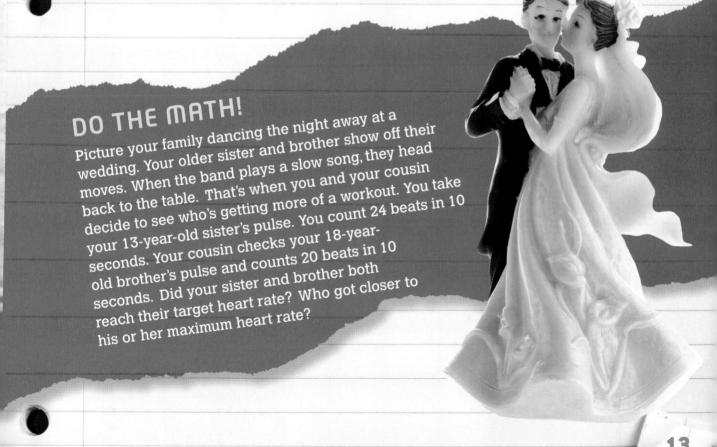

DO THE MATH!

Picture your family dancing the night away at a wedding. Your older sister and brother show off their moves. When the band plays a slow song, they head back to the table. That's when you and your cousin decide to see who's getting more of a workout. You take your 13-year-old sister's pulse. You count 24 beats in 10 seconds. Your cousin checks your 18-year-old brother's pulse and counts 20 beats in 10 seconds. Did your sister and brother both reach their target heart rate? Who got closer to his or her maximum heart rate?

HOP TO IT!

Quick—grab a potato sack! Tia and Tess are doing a potato-sack race with several of their friends. For this relay race, the group is divided into two teams. Players hop between a pair of cones spaced 25 feet (7.6 m) apart. Each player makes a round-trip before the next person on the team starts. Whichever team finishes first wins!

Tia and Tess are on opposite teams. They're also the final two people to hop. Tess begins four seconds ahead of Tia. She moves about 10 inches (25 centimeters) every time she hops. Her speed is about 1 foot (30 cm) per second.

By the time Tia gets going, Tess is almost 4 feet (1.2 m) past the starting line. Tia is determined to catch up, though! She clears about 9 inches (23 cm) per hop. She hops nearly 18 times in 10 seconds.

Yet, after reaching the second cone, Tia feels a little tired. So she slows down a bit during her return trip. The distance Tia covers per hop remains the same. But now she only hops half as fast. Meanwhile, Tess's speed on her way back is identical to her speed during the first half of the lap. **Based on their speeds, which friend will hop to victory in the potato-sack race? How far behind will the loser be?** (Hint: speed = distance ÷ time.)

STEPPING UP THE PACE

Carl feels as if he's been on his feet all day! He doesn't mind, though. He needs to keep moving if he hopes to win the step contest. A few weeks ago, Carl and his mom decided to get into better shape. So they began wearing pedometers. A pedometer counts someone's steps. This electronic device can be clipped to a waistband or a belt.

Pedometers help people figure out if they're walking as much as fitness experts recommend. Adults should be taking close to 8,500 steps per day. Kids—who tend to be more active than adults—should aim for about 12,000 steps per day.

Carl and Mom plan to wear the pedometers for eight weeks. By week 4, Carl is doing 10,000 steps per day. Mom's count is 9,000 steps per day. They decide to make things more interesting with a little contest.

Carl and Mom aim to increase their daily step count by 10 percent each week. By week 8, they'll see who's closer to achieving this goal. If Mom wins, Carl has to walk the family dog for eight weeks. If Carl wins, Mom has to do it. If Mom and Carl tie, they'll take turns walking Fluffy.

At the end of week 8, Mom is doing 12,000 steps per day. Meanwhile, Carl is up to 15,000 steps per day. **Who will walk Fluffy for the next eight weeks?**

DO THE MATH!

As you walk around your neighborhood, imagine that 100 steps on your pedometer = 1 mile (1.6 km) on an imaginary trail. Your destination on this pretend trail is Disney World—465 miles (748 km) from your house. You hope to make it there in five days. Let's say you started at 9,100 steps per day on day 1. The following two days, you were up to 9,300 steps per day. Yesterday, or day 4, you decreased to 8,900 steps per day. (You were a little less active than usual because you had a headache.) To get to Disney World by this evening, what should your pedometer read by the end of day 5?

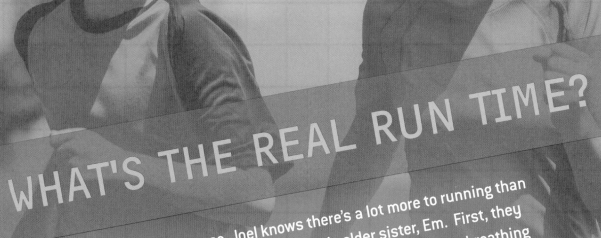

WHAT'S THE REAL RUN TIME?

Ready, set, run! Of course, Joel knows there's a lot more to running than that. Every Thursday afternoon, he runs with his older sister, Em. First, they do a warm-up. It includes a few minutes of light jogging, as well as breathing and stretching exercises. The warm-up gets their bodies ready for a period of increased activity.

At the end of their run, Joel and Em also jog and stretch to cool down. This eases their bodies into a slower, more restful state. The warm-up and cool-down help runners balance fitness with safety. Still, these steps take up a little extra time.

A few days ago, Em was elected president of the student council. It's great news, but meetings are Thursday afternoons! That means Joel and Em have to reschedule their weekly run.

Em suggests running Saturday mornings instead. Joel's OK with the switch. He just has to leave enough time to make it to his art class by 10:00 a.m. Joel guesses he'll need 20 minutes to shower and change. Afterward, Em is willing to drive him to class. She thinks she'll be able to get him there in five to 10 minutes, depending on traffic.

Normally, Joel and Em run 1.5 miles (2.4 km). The run itself, not counting the warm-up and the cool-down, takes about 15 minutes. When they warm up, they spend about one minute doing breathing exercises. They jog for roughly two minutes and stretch for two to three minutes. Then they do the same amount of jogging and stretching at the end of their run.

If Joel and Em run Saturdays, what time will they need to start warming up?

DO THE MATH!

You and your family are spending a day at the lake. Your sister challenges you to a race: a lap between two buoys spaced about 100 feet (30 m) apart. Since you're a member of your school swim team, you're confident you'll win. During your last meet, you swam the 50-yard (46 m) backstroke in 32 seconds. Today, you swim from one buoy to the next and then back in 51 seconds. You beat your sister's time, but how about your own? Was your speed faster or slower than it was at your last swim meet? (Hints: 1 yard = 3 feet [0.9 m]; speed = distance traveled ÷ the time it takes to travel that distance.)

SAME OLD, SAME OLD?

Who enjoys doing the same thing over and over? Not Zach! He's all about being physically active at least 60 minutes every day. But Zach likes to mix things up. If possible, he switches between the types of activities he does.

Aunt Sue—who works as a fitness trainer—recommends intense exercise three days a week. Moderate exercise is best for the rest of the week. Target heart rate during intense exercise = 70 to 85 percent of a person's maximum heart rate. Meanwhile, target heart rate during moderate exercise = 50 to 70 percent of a person's maximum heart rate.

Aunt Sue likes the idea of alternating both types of exercise. That way, Zach's body has a chance to rest and recover between intense workouts. Aunt Sue even offers to help him track his heart rate during various physical activities. This will make it easier to plan Zach's weekly workout schedule.

Together, Zach and Aunt Sue create the following list:

Zach's Heart Rate during Different Physical Activities	
Biking (alone)	161 bpm
Biking (with little sister)	120 bpm
Hiking uphill	165 bpm
Jumping rope	155 bpm
Playing tennis (doubles)	130 bpm
Playing tennis (singles)	159 bpm
Running	166 bpm
Swimming laps	164 bpm
Walking quickly	144 bpm

Zach is nine years old. **If he hikes up a hilly trail Monday, what activities should he choose from on Tuesday?**

AS MANY PUSH-UPS AS POSSIBLE

Normally, Wes isn't wild about push-ups. Neither are his friends, Amir and Anne. Today, however, they're participating in the Presidential Youth Fitness Program (PYFP). Schools across the nation use this program to teach kids about fitness and exercise.

Part of PYFP involves different physical fitness tests. This afternoon, Mr. Kwan, the gym teacher, announces that the fourth graders will be doing push-ups. He plans to track how many each student can do in one minute.

Before they get started, Mr. Kwan divides the class into three groups. Amir is in Group A, Anne is in Group B, and Wes is in Group C. There are six students per group.

Mr. Kwan explains he'll figure out the average number of push-ups each group can do. **The average number of push-ups per group = the total number of push-ups per group ÷ the number of students per group.**

The winning group will get to decide what sport everyone plays in gym next week! Amir's group wants to do floor hockey. Anne's group votes for volleyball. Wes and Group C have their hearts set on flag football.

Mr. Kwan records results in the table below. Wes is the last one to go! **How many push-ups must he do in one minute for his team to to win? If he does fewer than that amount, which sport will the class be playing next week?** Round to the nearest whole push-up.

Push-Ups per Minute in Mr. Kwan's Fourth-Grade Gym Class					
Group A		Group B		Group C	
Amir	32	Ethan	38	Ben	34
Caleb	20	Anne	19	Cara	17
Janelle	21	Natalia	18	Maya	20
Lexi	17	Josh	35	Nico	41
Marco	32	Cassie	21	Olivia	20
Yola	21	Lin	19	Wes	?
Group average:		Group average:		Group average:	

FOOD OR FUEL?

C'mon, kick the ball! Kim was hoping she'd do just that and score a few goals for her soccer team today. Instead, she feels as if she's ready to head back to bed! Kim got plenty of sleep last night. So why is she dragging herself across the field?

Coach Ada asks what Kim ate for breakfast. Kim tells her she was running late this morning. So she only had time to grab a banana on her way out the door. Aha! Coach Ada suspects Kim's meal plan might be part of the problem. It sounds as though Kim didn't take in enough calories before the game. Coach Ada explains that calories are units of energy found in food. They fuel a person's body with energy the same way gas powers a car. People burn, or use up, calories during physical activity.

Consuming calories that don't get burned causes weight gain. Yet eating too few calories leads to fatigue and other health problems. Without enough energy, it's hard to be physically active.

Coach Ada and Kim look online and learn that a banana contains 105 calories. Someone Kim's age (10) should be eating about 1,600 calories a day. Coach Ada suggests getting about 25 percent of that amount during breakfast.

The following Saturday, Kim leaves enough time to bite into more than a banana. All she has to do is pick what to put on her plate. One possibility is a whole-grain muffin (180 calories) and ½ cup (73 grams) of blueberries (40 calories). A second option is a whole-wheat pita (170 calories) filled with scrambled egg whites (90 calories). No matter what she eats, Kim plans to have a glass of low-fat milk (100 calories) on the side.

Does either breakfast option fit Coach Ada's recommendations? If not, will adding links of turkey sausage (60 calories each) help either of them measure up to the ideal amount of calories? Round up to the nearest whole turkey sausage link.

TAKE A HIKE!

Who's up for a hike? Harry is! On November 8, he'll be hiking 5 miles (8 km) with his Cub Scout troop. But Harry knows he shouldn't wait until the last minute to get in shape for this adventure. He has no experience hiking. That's why Mr. Cortez, the scoutmaster, tells him to plan ahead and start training early.

Mr. Cortez wants Harry to do a practice hike of 1 mile (1.6 km) during his first week of training. Then he should hike 0.5 miles (0.8 km) farther the next week, 0.5 miles beyond that the third week, and so on. Eventually, Harry should be comfortable hiking 5 miles (8 km).

Yet that's only part of Harry's training. Mr. Cortez says that Harry should also get used to wearing a heavy backpack. By November, he should be able to carry up to 20 percent of his own body weight. Harry weighs 70 pounds (32 kilograms).

A week after reaching his target distance, Harry should add a backpack to his training routine. Mr. Cortez says it should weigh about 2 pounds (907 g) at first. Harry should keep adding 2 pounds per week until he's close to his maximum backpack weight. By November 1, he should be carrying a load that's within about 1 pound (454 g) of that.

Harry begins training on July 19. He hikes with one of his parents every Saturday. **If he stays on schedule, will he be ready by November 8?** Refer to a calendar if you need to!

DO THE MATH!

You're getting ready for a 3.5-mile (5.6 km) hike with your family. You know you should pack plenty of water. Mom says to bring 1 liter for each mile you'll be hiking. But since it's your first time hitting the trails, she doesn't want to overload you. So Mom tells you to just fill and pack your own thermos. It holds 24 fluid ounces. She'll carry your additional water in her extra canteen. If necessary, your dad can fill his extra canteen too. Each canteen holds up to 2 quarts. Will your mom's extra canteen be enough, or should your dad pack his too? (Hints: 1 liter = 34 fluid ounces; 1 quart = 32 fluid ounces.)

READY, SET, HULA-HOOP!

Is your heart pounding yet? If not, swim some laps, kick a soccer ball, or dance to the music! First, though, warm up by solving a few final problems.

Ready to raise funds for fitness? You're about to participate in a fund-raiser to help build a new school gym. During the past few weeks, you have collected pledges from family, friends, and neighbors. The pledges are promises to pay a certain amount of money based on how well you perform different fitness challenges.

Challenge No. 1 is all about Hula-Hooping. You need to Hula-Hoop as long as possible without letting your hoop drop to the ground. Seven of the people on your pledge list have promised $1.00 for every second you manage to do this.

You'll have three chances to Hula-Hoop. Your score will be the average of these three times. Can you make it a whole minute? Not quite—54 seconds, 48 seconds, and 51 seconds. Not bad for a beginner, though! **What's your score for the Hula-Hoop competition?**

For Challenge No. 2, you have to crab walk a complete lap between two cones. The cones are spaced 15 feet (4.6 m) apart. Nine people on your pledge list have offered to give you 50¢ for every foot you crawl in the last 10 seconds. You finish your lap in 35 seconds, going the same speed the whole time. **What is your crab-walking speed?**

For Challenge No. 3, you must do as many jumping jacks as possible in two minutes. Five people on your pledge list have agreed to pay 25¢ per jumping jack. OK, feet together! Arms out to your sides! And . . . go! One minute into Challenge No. 3, the volunteer timing you tells you your total so far—62. You're a little tired during the second half. So you end up doing five fewer jumping jacks than you did in the first half. **How much money will you collect for Challenge No. 3? What is the total amount you have raised for a new gym?**

Answer Key

Page 7 Claire is doing an average of 45 minutes of physical activity per day. (10 + 15 + 25 = 50 mins.; 5 + 15 + 5 + 10 = 35 mins.; 5 + 20 + 15 + 10 = 50 mins.; 50 + 35 + 50 = 135 mins.; 135 mins. ÷ 3 days = 45 mins./day)
Claire is getting 75 percent of her recommended activity. (45 mins./day ÷ 60 mins./day = 0.75, or 75 percent)

Do the Math!
You have walked up or down 216 stair steps. (4 floors × 12 steps = 48 steps; 6 floors × 12 steps = 72 steps; 2 floors × 12 steps = 24 steps; 3 floors × 12 steps = 36 steps; 3 floors × 12 steps = 36 steps; 48 + 72 + 24 + 36 + 36 = 216 steps)

Page 10 Marc and Nina have walked 2.4 miles (3.9 km). (¼ mi. × 2 = ½ mi./block; ½ mi./block × 4 blocks = 2 mi.; 28 ft. [width of a street] × 5 streets = 140 ft.; 315 ft. [width of a block/gap between streets] × 3 = 945 ft; 945 ft. + 140 ft. = 1,085 ft.; 1,085 ft. ÷ 5,280 ft./mi. = 0.2 mi.; 0.2 mi. + 2 mi. + 0.2 mi. = 2.4 mi.)

Page 13 Dancing is a safe, effective way for Gwen to be physically active. (220 bpm − 10 = 210 bpm [max. heart rate]; 50 percent = 0.50; 85 percent = 0.85; 210 bpm × 0.50 = 105 bpm [min. target heart rate]; 210 bpm × 0.85 = 179 bpm [max. target heart rate]; 25 beats × 6 = 150 bpm; 150 bpm ≥ 105 bpm; 150 bpm ≤ 179 bpm)

Do the Math!
Your sister and brother both reached their target heart rate. (50 percent = 0.50; 85 percent = 0.85; 220 bpm − 13 = 207 bpm [sister's max. rate]; 207 bpm × 0.50 = 104 bpm; 207 bpm × 0.85 = 176 bpm; 24 beats × 6 = 144 bpm [sister's pulse]; 144 bpm ≥ 104 bpm; 144 bpm ≤ 176 bpm; 220 bpm − 18 = 202 bpm [brother's max. rate]; 202 bpm × 0.50 = 101 bpm; 202 bpm × 0.85 = 172 bpm; 20 beats × 6 = 120 bpm [brother's pulse]; 120 bpm ≥ 101 bpm; 120 bpm ≤ 172 bpm)
Your sister got closer to her maximum heart rate. (144 bpm ÷ 207 bpm = 0.695 or .70 or 70 percent of your sister's max. heart rate; 120 bpm ÷ 202 bpm = 0.594 or 0.59 or 59 percent of your brother's max. heart rate; 70 percent > 59 percent)

Page 15 Tess will hop to victory. (25 ft. × 12 in./ft. = 300 in. between cones; 300 in. × 2 trips between cones = 600 in.; 18 hops ÷ 10 secs. = 1.8 hops/secs. [Tia's speed for the first half]; 9 in./hop × 1.8 hops/secs. = 16.2 in./sec.; 300 in. ÷ 16.2 in./secs. = 18.5 secs. [Tia's time for the first half]; 16.2 in./secs. ÷ 2 = 8.1 in./secs. [Tia's speed for the second half]; 300 in. ÷ 8.1 in./sec. = 37 secs. [Tia's time for the second half]; 18.5 secs. + 37 secs. = 55.5 secs. [Tia's total time]; 600 in. ÷ 12 in./secs. [Tess's speed for both halves] = 50 secs.; 50 < 55.5)
Tia finishes 9.5 seconds behind Tess. (4 ft. [Tess's head start] ÷ 1 ft./sec. [Tess's speed] = 4 secs.; 55.5 secs. [Tia's time] − 50 secs. [Tess's time] = 5.5 secs.; 5.5.secs. + 4 secs. = 9.5 secs.)

Page 17 Mom will walk Fluffy for the next eight weeks. (Carl: 10,000 steps/day [week 4] × 0.10 = 1,000 steps/day; 1,000 steps/day + 10,000 steps/day = 11,000 steps/day [week 5 goal]; 11,000 steps/day × 0.10 = 1,100 steps/day; 1,100 steps/day + 11,000 steps/day = 12,100 steps/day [week 6 goal]; 12,100 steps/day × 0.10 = 1,210 steps/day; 1,210 steps/day + 12,100 steps/day = 13,310 steps/day [week 7 goal]; 13,310 steps/day × 0.10 = 1,331 steps/day; 1,331 steps/day + 13,310 steps/day = 14,641 steps/day [week 8 goal]; 14,641 steps/day < 15,000 steps/day [actual week 8 steps/day]; Mom: 9,000 steps/day × 0.10 = 900 steps/day; 900 steps/day + 9,000 steps/day = 9,900 steps/day [week 5 goal]; 9,900 steps/day × 0.10 = 990 steps/day; 990 steps/day + 9,900 steps/day = 10,890 steps/day [week 6 goal]; 10,890 steps/day × 0.10 = 1,089 steps/day; 1,089 steps/day + 10,890 steps/day = 11,979 steps/day [week 7 goal]; 11,979 steps/day × 0.10 = 1,197.9, or 1,198 steps/day; 1,198 steps/day + 11,979 steps/day = 13,177 steps/day [week 8 goal]; 13,177 steps/day > 12,000 steps/day [actual week 8 steps/day]])

Do the Math!
Your pedometer should read 9,900 steps per day by the end of day 5. (9,100 steps + 9,300 steps + 9,300 steps

+ 8,900 steps = 36,600 steps; 36,600 steps ÷ 100 steps/mi. = 366 mi.; 465 mi. − 366 mi. = 99 mi. remaining; 99 × 100 steps/mi. = 9,900 steps/day)

Page 19 Joel and Em will need to start warming up at 9:04 a.m. (1 min. + 2 mins. + 3 mins. + 15 mins. + 2 min. + 3 mins. + 20 mins. + 10 mins. = 56 mins.; 10:00 a.m. − 56 mins. = 9:04 a.m.)

Do the Math!
Your speed was faster than at your last swim meet. (100 ft. [distance between buoys] × 2 times swimming between buoys = 200 ft.; 200 ft. ÷ 3 ft./yd. = 66.7 yd., or 67 yd.; 67 yd. ÷ 51 secs. = 1.3 yd./secs.; 50 yd. ÷ 32 secs. = 1.6 yd./secs.; 1.6 yd./secs. < 1.3 yd./secs.)

Page 21 Zach should choose from biking (with his sister), playing tennis (doubles), and walking quickly. (50 percent = 0.50; 70 percent = 0.70; 85 percent = 0.85; 220 bpm − 9 years old = 211 bpm [max. heart rate]; 211 bpm × 0.50 = 105.5 bpm, or 106 bpm [min. moderate target]; 211 bpm × 0.70 = 147.7 bpm, or 148 bpm [max. moderate target and min. intense target]; 211 bpm × 0.85 = 179.4 bpm, or 179 bpm [max. intense target]; Monday = intense exercise; Tuesday should = moderate exercise)

Page 23 Wes must do 24 push-ups. (Group A: 32 + 20 + 21 + 17 + 32 + 21 = 143; 143 ÷ 6 = 23.8, or 24 push-ups; Group B: 38 + 19 + 18 + 35 + 21 + 19 = 150; 150 ÷ 6 = 25 push-ups; 25 > 24; Group C must average ≥ 26 push-ups to win; Group C: 34 + 17 + 20 + 41 + 20 = 132; 26 × 6 = 156 push-ups [total needed to win]; 156 − 132 = 24) If he does fewer than 24, the class will be playing volleyball. (25 [Group B average] > 24 [Group A average])

Page 25 Neither breakfast fits Coach Ada's recommendations. (25 percent = 0.25; 0.25 × 1,600 cal. = 400 cal.; 180 cal. + 40 cal. + 100 cal. = 320 cal.; 320 cal. < 400 cal.; 170 cal. + 90 cal. + 100 cal. = 360 cal.; 360 cal. < 400 cal.) Adding two links of turkey sausage to Kim's first meal option or one link of turkey sausage to her second meal option will work. (400 cal. − 320 cal. = 80 cal.; 80 cal. ÷ 60 cal./link = 1.33, or 2 sausage links; 400 cal. − 360 cal. = 40 cal.; 40 cal. ÷ 60 cal./link = 0.67, or 1 sausage link)

Page 27 If he keeps to the schedule, Harry will be ready by November 8. (20 percent = 0.20; 0.20 × 70 lb. = 14 lb. [max. weight of backpack]; July 19 to Nov. 1 = 16 weeks; 1 mi. [week 1] + 0.5 mi. = 1.5 mi.; 1.5 mi. + 0.5 mi. = 2 mi.; 2 mi. + 0.5 mi. = 2.5 mi.; 2.5 mi. + 0.5 mi. = 3 mi.; 3 mi. + 0.5 mi. = 3.5 mi.; 3.5 mi. + 0.5 mi. = 4 mi.; 4 mi. + 0.5 mi. = 4.5 mi. 4.5 mi. + 0.5 mi. = 5 mi. = target distance; week 10 = add 2 lb. backpack; 2 lb. + 2 lb. = 4 lb.; 4 lb. + 2 lb. = 6 lb.; 6 lb. + 2 lb. = 8 lb.; 8 lb. + 2 lb. = 10 lb.; 10 lb. + 2 lb. = 12 lb.; 12 lb. + 2 lb. = 14 lb. [weight for week 16])

Do the Math!
Your mom's extra canteen will not be enough. Your dad should pack his too. (3.5 mi. ÷ 1 L/mile = 3.5 L; 3.5 L × 34 fl. oz./L = 119 fl. oz.; 119 fl. oz. − 24 fl. oz. = 95 fl. oz.; 2 qt. × 32 fl. oz./qt. = 64 fl. oz.; 64 fl. oz. < 95 fl. oz.)

Page 29 **Make Math Happen!**
Your Hula-Hoop score is 51 seconds. (54 secs. + 48 secs. + 51 secs. = 153 secs.; 153 secs. ÷ 3 = 51 secs.)
Your crab-walking speed is 0.9 feet per second. (15 ft. × 2 = 30 ft.; 30 ft. ÷ 35 secs. = 0.86 ft./sec, or 0.9 ft./sec.)
You are due to collect $148.75 for Challenge No. 3. (62 − 5 = 57; 62 + 57 = 119 jumping jacks; 25¢ = 0.25; 0.25 × 119 = $29.75 per person; $29.75 × 5 people = $148.75)
You have raised a total of $546.25. ($1/sec. you Hula-Hoop × 51 secs. = $51 per person; $51 × 7 people = $357 [for Challenge No. 1]; 50¢ per foot = $0.50; 0.9 ft./sec. × 10 secs. = 9 ft.; 9 ft. × $0.50/ft. = $4.50 per person; $4.50 × 9 people = $40.50 [for Challenge No. 2]; $357 + $40.50 + $148.75 = $546.25)

Glossary

average: the sum of a group of numbers divided by the size of that group

calorie: a unit of energy found in food

intense: extreme or producing a strong effect

moderate: not extreme or producing an average effect

pedometer: an electronic device that counts someone's steps

pulse: the rhythmic movement of arteries as the heart pumps blood throughout the body

speed: distance traveled divided by the time it takes to travel that distance

Further Information

Cleary, Brian P. *A Second, a Minute, a Week with Days in It: A Book about Time.* Minneapolis: Millbrook Press, 2013. Take a fun, lighthearted look at several math concepts involving time that are also applicable to fitness.

IXL Learning: Third Grade
http://www.ixl.com/math/grade-3
This site includes examples and practice problems to help you perfect your growing math skills.

Marsico, Katie. *Ball Game Math.* Minneapolis: Lerner Publications, 2015. Explore how math plays a role in many sports that go hand in hand with physical fitness.

The President's Challenge—Choose a Challenge: Presidential Youth Fitness Program (PYFP)
https://www.presidentschallenge.org/challenge/pyfp.shtml
Find out more about how the PYFP helps kids learn about fitness and the best ways to get moving.

Index